THE SHADOWS OF MY SOUL

poems by LEON THORNTON, JR.

TATE PUBLISHING
AND **ENTERPRISES**, LLC

The Shadows of My Soul
Copyright © 2016 by Leon Thornton, Jr. All rights reserved.

No part of this publication may be reproduced, stored in a retrieval system or transmitted in any way by any means, electronic, mechanical, photocopy, recording or otherwise without the prior permission of the author except as provided by USA copyright law.

This book is designed to provide accurate and authoritative information with regard to the subject matter covered. This information is given with the understanding that neither the author nor Tate Publishing, LLC is engaged in rendering legal, professional advice. Since the details of your situation are fact dependent, you should additionally seek the services of a competent professional.

The opinions expressed by the author are not necessarily those of Tate Publishing, LLC.

Published by Tate Publishing & Enterprises, LLC
127 E. Trade Center Terrace | Mustang, Oklahoma 73064 USA
1.888.361.9473 | www.tatepublishing.com

Tate Publishing is committed to excellence in the publishing industry. The company reflects the philosophy established by the founders, based on Psalm 68:11,
"The Lord gave the word and great was the company of those who published it."

Book design copyright © 2016 by Tate Publishing, LLC. All rights reserved.
Cover design by Jim Villaflores
Interior design by Richell Balansag

Published in the United States of America

ISBN: 978-1-68270-538-4
Poetry / General
15.10.29

Acknowledgments

First and foremost, I want to thank God for giving me life, love, family, talent, and, hopefully, an audience with whom to share my talents.

This book is dedicated to my wife, Kimberly H. Thornton (a.k.a. Sweets). We have been married for nineteen years! And she has been my friend, lover, and dedicated coparent to our sons for twenty-six years. I admire her intelligence and beauty. Although our stars do not always align, I thank her for opening her heart to me so many moons ago. Kim knows my passion and love for her runs deeper and longer than the Nile River.

I thank my sons, Leon Jabari Hanif Thornton and Alexander Nakuru Dia Thornton, for their honesty, kindness, and patience as I learn to be a better father. Thank God for giving us two wonderful and handsome sons. They should be comforted in knowing their parents love them deeply and wish them peace, joy, and success in their many endeavors.

With bountiful love and admiration, I thank my mother, Mary Kee Thornton. Whenever I doubted myself or was feeling down, my mother would always try to lift my spirits and help me see things with a positive perspective. She often told me that if I could not talk to her or family, then go to God because He always listens. And she was right.

This book is also dedicated to my sister, Sherna (pronounced Sher-nay). We spent a lot of time together when I was much younger because she was more than my sister. She was my babysitter, confidant, friend, and very first poetry critic, editor, and fan. I thank her for encouraging me to put pen to pad and breathe life into my abstract thoughts. I truly wish I could go back in time and support her as much as she has supported me.

I would like to thank my other sister, Susette (a.k.a. Suzy Q). While growing up on Martin Luther King Drive and Crowell Street, in Hempstead, New York, I would intentionally irritate or embarrass her. And, in turn, she harassed and bullied the hell out of me in order to, as she often says, "Toughen me up!" Still, like a big sister, she always looked out for me. Although we rarely saw eye-to-eye as children, as adults we have grown closer and share a common Virgo bond that will never be broken.

I remember not that long ago at the tender age of five watching my brother, Carl, sing onstage during a concert at Hempstead High School. Everyone was screaming and shouting, and, I thought they were yelling at him out of anger! My mom assured me they were shouting out of joy because his wonderful voice excited them. Watching Carl pursue his dreams—on stage—inspired me to walk out on faith and pursue my dreams as a writer.

I would also like to dedicate my book to Leon Thornton Sr. (a.k.a. Pop). Pop taught me to be resilient, resourceful, courageous, and to speak up in order to be heard. For the first twelve years of my life we were extremely tight. He was more than a father—he was my protector, brother, and friend. But eventually, tumultuous life events caused an emotional chasm that separated us for years. At times, I was afraid to tell him what emotional scars lay unhealed on my wounded heart. Instead, I bottled up my feelings and later wrote them down as best I could. (So it goes without saying that these poems are a window to my soul. And as he turns each page, he will surely open the window wider and wider.) Some of these poems may seem bitter, angry, and sullen, but he should not be afraid to grab them, instead of deflecting them, as they leap off the pages. I truly hope he will understand that, for me, writing is the dream that was deferred and it is the path that I should have taken long ago. Although Pop pushed me down a different path for security and financial gain, he did what he thought was best out of love. For that, I can truly say—besides my two boys—there is no man I have ever loved more than my father.

I would be remiss if I failed to thank my extended family:

Thank you, Sarah V. George (a.k.a. mother-in-law), for letting me live with you and your daughter, Kim, when I was homeless, jobless, and penniless.

Thanks to my nephews, Blaise Gibson Jr. and Brandon Gibson, Big Blaise (my brother-in-law), Kerry and Alicia K. Vaughan, Carmela, Terence and Lydia Peavy, Vivian Liley, Donald Liley, Welton Liley Jr., Danny Liley, Tavis Liley, the late Michael Liley, the late Uncle Welton and Aunt Evelyn Liley, Uncle George and Aunt Peggy Kee, Kevin Kee and George Kee Jr., Anton Young, my late uncles Otis, Frank, and Larry Kee, Ms. Barbara Henderson, Dana and Melodie Jackson, Aunt "Ginny" Young, Aunt Dora Lee Kee, Aunt Neat Kee, Aunt Betty Denny, Aunt Katheryne, Aunt Deloris Buggs, Aunt Theresa Craig, Aunt Lorraine Hudson, and the late Aunt Bernice Alexander, and all my other aunts, uncles, and cousins from California, Georgia, New York, Maryland, Mississippi, North Carolina, Texas, Wisconsin, and wherever else our DNA resides. Without your prayers, support, guidance, admiration, humor, toughness, and love during my youth and adulthood, my mind would be absent of fond memories.

Thanks to Mr. William "Chip" Miller for bringing African American literature to life at York College of Pennsylvania. Your energy and passion was quite contagious and inspiring!

I would like to thank specific members of the acquisitions team, Lyn Pacquiao and Jesse Atienza for reaching out to me via telephone and e-mail.

And, of course, I appreciate the wonderful and thought-provoking conversations with Trinity Tate-Edgerton. Whether she knows it or not, the comfort level I developed with her during our first conference call is truly one of the reasons I decided to move forward with my manuscript and work with Tate Publishing.

I would like to thank Michelle Cabaral, Michael Aggarao, Julius Ramas, Jedd Dedrick Uy, and others involved in the production and marketing of this book. You helped me reach my goal—to publish my very first poetry book. I applaud your efforts!

To all my poetry professors, the late great Langston Hughes, Paul Laurence Dunbar, Dudley Randall, Walt Whitman, Sterling Brown, Countee Cullen, Maya Angelou, Gwendolyn Brooks, Imamu Amiri Baraka, Robert Frost, and the remarkable Edgar Alan Poe, thank you for the countless hours of reading and training at home, school, college, libraries, bookstores, doctor's offices, parks, in cars, on ships, trains, and airplanes. Your poems and writings had (and have) a tremendous impact on my life and my craft. If I had not read your words, I would not have found my own voice.

Lastly, I would like to thank you, the readers, for purchasing my book of poems. As you affix your eyes to the words on these pages, I sincerely hope my poems awaken your innermost thoughts and deepest emotions. Should you happen to feel the depths of despair, perhaps some of my poems can wrap their sympathetic arms around you and move you from tears to smiles (from sadness to joy). I hope you find solace in knowing I too suffer self-doubt, sorrow, pain, and misfortune. But rest assure, I know there is a light that shines bright within me that refuses to allow myself to wallow in pity for too long—because there is so much life to live, so much happiness to dance in, so many good times to create and share and enjoy. There are so many possibilities to mature and grow as a person and as human being, so many chances to turn your frowns upside down, and so many more opportunities to use your handkerchief to wipe away someone else's tears. Readers, if you feel you are not loved by your family or friends or neighbors or coworkers or strangers or even yourselves, know that you are loved by God.

Contents

PART I: SHADOWS OF MY SOUL

Me, Dear Lord!... 17

Jesus, I Must Not Travel Alone!...................................... 18

Raindrops of Pain 19

At My Hands 20

A Rat Am I... 22

Empty Life 24

Alone Am I.. 26

Selfless War 27

Homeless 29

Despair 30

Sea of Shame 32

Ship A-Comin'.. 35

The Shadows of My Soul 36

Part II: As the Sun Retires

Diverge! 41

City Square 43

Crocodile Tears 45

Cascading Light 47

Whispers of the Wild 49

As the Sun Retires 52

Part III: Many Moons Ago

Wars 57

Number A2234 60

Wa-Tu Wa-Le Wa-Mefika 62

Weeping Willow 66

Many Moons Ago 68

Part IV: A Candle Lit Above the Trees

The Sun Sets on Many Hearts 73

Shattered Heart 74

Little Bluebird 76

Lieben 78

A Candle Lit Above the Trees 80

Part V: She Drank from My Cup

She Drank from My Cup 85
A Steady Beat 86
Valentine's Forgotten Memory 87
She Is Not My Wife 89
Remnants of Sex 91
She Sits Quiet and Still 92
To Mock the Raven 94
Shimmering Blue Eyes 95

Part VI: Purple Prisms of Pain

Possession 99
Please Don't Go! 101
Distant Sounds of Drunken Laughter 103
Future Becomes Present Becomes Past 104
Eyes Closed to the Light 106
Reflection 108
I Was Born Not Out of Love 109
Purple Prisms of Pain 111

PART VII: BEYOND THE BLUE MOON

Crescendo 115
Sand and Pebble 116
Silver Shadows... 117
Verlanda—You Were Taken Much Too Soon 118
Verlanda 2—If You'd Known Her................................ 120
River of Light 122
Beyond the Blue Moon.. 124

PART I

Shadows of My Soul

Me, Dear Lord!

O' Lord,
I been feelin' mighty lonesome.
O' Lord,
I been feelin' mighty scared.

The devil is out
To get me—

      Me, Dear Lord!

The sinner that I am.

March 27, 1987

Jesus, I Must Not Travel Alone!

My mind is obscure
And bewildered;
My heart is as hard
As brick and stone.
If ever I should
Travel the right road
Again, Jesus—
> I must not travel alone—
>> *Jesus, I must not travel alone!*
> March 27, 1987

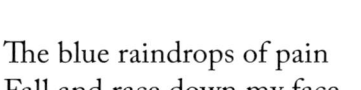

Raindrops of Pain

The blue raindrops of pain
Fall and race down my face,
Drenched in intensity!
Dare I hide from disgrace?

I stand naked beneath
A gloomy, gray sky.
I loom in darkness—
I don't know why.

There is a forlorn tree laying in my path,
Uprooted from its foundation.

That's ironic! It's symbolic of my bleak life—
Uprooted!
    and headed
        toward Hell's
            blazing abyss,

The eternal womb of damnation.

At My Hands

No one could even hear
The whimper that softly sailed
Across a silent wind,

Nor the snap of soft bones
Swiftly between one's
Powerful deadly grip.

No one would ever find,
So carefully scattered outside,
Pieces of my newborn puzzle.

There were no clues, except,
The faint cry that echoed
In my aching head—

And the deep dark
Stain of one's blood
That I left behind,

Next to the toy rattle
In the baby's crib—
I killed my baby!—

At my hands, my baby died!

Revised August 20, 2015

A Rat Am I

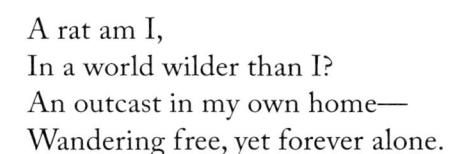

A rat am I,
In a world wilder than I?
An outcast in my own home—
Wandering free, yet forever alone.

> Far be it for me to share grievances
> With a world that is as empty as I.
> Far be it for me, on a searing whim,
> To dare shed light on a dreary dream.

I search for guidance on a lighthouse dock,
Subtly spying nothing but rocks.
And though each rock is unique, firm, and true,
Rocks can be lost in an ocean of blues.

> Futility rings fiercely in my ears
> From cracked chiming bells of arguments near.
> Even if headstones turned in beds of green,
> Nothing's more troubling than one's fading dreams.

Harsher than harsh, colder than cold—
My eyes weep blood as black as coal.
I live in fear—far from being bold!
I am a sewer rat who's all alone.

Empty Life

Hard is the core of my heart:
i have lost my wife in strife.
my baby boy was a stillborn—
his baby-blue room
        remains empty…

Weak are my appendages:
i do nothing with my hands—i am no artist;
i do nothing with my feet—i am no dancer;
i do nothing with my lips—i am no orator.
        i am worthless…

Fragile is the crater of my mind:
i never climbed the corporate ladder—
i slipped on every rung!
Fear pulls back the reins of my
        galloping horse…

Troubled is the center of my soul:
no gods to worship, no friends to speak of,
no road on which to travel—
i am stuck at the
       crossroads of life.

Alone Am I

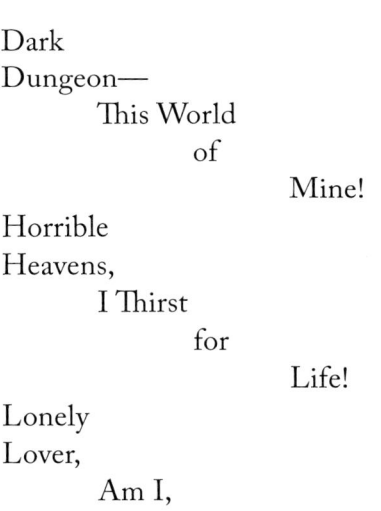

Dark
Dungeon—
      This World
            of
                  Mine!
Horrible
Heavens,
     I Thirst
          for
               Life!
Lonely
Lover,
     Am I,
         Who
              Dances

Naked beneath the moon and stars.

Selfless War

I am waging a war within myself—
Belligerence prevents the control
Of each fiber of my being. Cells oft
Burn intensely from the torrid pool
Of flames that are ignited by a fool's
      Sad soul,
              Mad soul…
Senseless rage is shortly diverted by
Solemness—unrequited love (alone)
Wreaked havoc on my loving heart by
Chiseling away pieces 'til all gone;
Except the core: a solid red stone
      Oh, my drumless heart
            Oh, my aching heart…
The bitter flavor of Vengeance's dirt
Would taste sweet right about now. But why
Pour salt on an aching, drumless heart,
Which yearns for golden drops of honey.

My sour soul is clearly bewildered—
        Sad soul,
                Mad soul…
Rage still lingers within.

Homeless

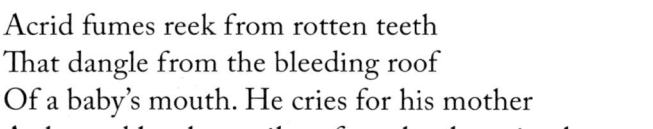

Acrid fumes reek from rotten teeth
That dangle from the bleeding roof
Of a baby's mouth. He cries for his mother
As he suckles the spoilage from her lactating breasts.

Cuddled up in a corner is a body,
Alone—sheltered from icy snowdrift by
An old crumpled, yellow *New York Times*—
"What a waste of a good newspaper!"

Armies of red ants besiege the carcass
Of an old man whose sightless
Eyes cannot see the stinging pain
That his flesh surely feels.

Swarthy, emaciated, stockingless legs struggle
Against a fierce freezing rain and brutal
Wind toward a destination not known,
Toward a warm, dry place never found.

Despair

I

Rings of white smoke circle his untidy gray
Crown. White stubble leaps off his pale cheeks. Hazy
Brown eyes feebly peer at his swarthy,
Wrinkled, arthritic hands—
    Their once powerful grip now lost.

II

Her visage, once pink and soft, is now
Rugged and worn. Her lips
Are chapped and yearn the warm
Subtle touch of manly lips.
She struggles across the street with her new home:
A cart full of dirty clothes, raggedy shoes, cheap perfume,
Plastic bags full of used beer bottles and soda cans
And a dark gray blanket, which she uses, often,
    To shield herself from her bleak existence.

III

His dingy, mangled clothes hang loosely
From his emaciated body.
He resembles a skeletal-ghost who dances drunkenly
In the streets, while beseeching cars
To hit him. But instead,
Cars avoid the glare of glazed black
Eyes rolling in his head.
So, he angrily screams and shouts
Vulgar words, as he limps
Toward oncoming traffic: "You
Mother———, mechanical whimps!
> You can't kill me anyway, 'cause I'm already dead!"

IV

Though their hearts still vigorously pump blood
And their pulses are steadfast and strong,
I wonder if I could ever lead their bleak, forlorn lives—
> Godforsaken, penniless, and alone.

Sea of Shame

The bright stars sparkle in the night sky.
Each casts its own individual, isolated light
Upon land and sea. While I stand firmly
On the earth beneath the swirling night
Sky, I gaze up at the white glitter. Suddenly
Out of the bright night appears an obscure image
Before me. I caught only a glimpse of this shadowy
Figure, floating on the surface of the sea. Though it's vague
Form blends in with the darkness, the glow
From the glittering white souls makes the large
Creature slightly distinguishable. It stands, so
Sullenly, slowly peeling her visage
Like the dried skin of an onion, oh!—
Revealing layer after layer of misery and anguish!
There [it] stands, so alone, so naked, so frail!
Beneath this creature's beautiful flesh
Lies an ugly truth: It's a woman who dwells

In a world of ignominy; she is worthless!
She is even ashamed of her personal
Attributes—ashamed of her life
And of her color! *Her color?* Her color!
What an indignity to herself, as well as
To her own kind!—I carefully watch this sister
Swim against a sea of guilt and shame, because
Presumably, she truly knows that her
Ignorant beliefs and feelings were the passed
Tragic errors of her ways; that they sever
Her from her own people. Unlike I, she has
No ground on which to stand. Her incognizance
And fruitless thoughts virtually thrust
Her from light to darkness; her ignorance,
Which may be the fault of her parents, must
Cast her down a sorrowful, spiraling staircase
Of shame forever, and ever, and ever. Thus,
The complexity of her actions and brain's impotence
Is sadly perplexing and bleak to me. It's too much
Of a dream to be real, yet, too real to be
A dream! While I contemplate her condition,
She quickly vanishes from existence, as though she
Has blended with the water and darkness. Awed
And bewildered, I gaze at the tranquil sea.
The white dust, scattered in the on

The painted sky, casts fragments of lonely
Light upon the surface of a murky ocean
That embraces the sullen sea. As I
Watch, mesmerized by the soft, rippling
Currents, suddenly an obscure,
Defaced image lurks out—*springs
Forth!*—from the depths of the deep sea, peers
At me with solemn eyes, then
Slowly sinks back beneath the surface of the
Sea of shame.

Ship A-Comin'

O' God:
>When will my ship sail in
>To port an' take me away?

O' God:
>When will my ship sail in
>To port an' lift my burdens today?

O' Bountiful God:
>When will my ship reel in
>Its anchor of mercy
>An' set forth with my soul?

O' Almighty God:
>When will my ship sail away
>An' take me to another world,
>One which I can truly call Home?

Summer of 1986

The Shadows of My Soul

The shadows of my soul
>   *Burden me,*
>   *Burden me!*
I seek no escape,
For if any exists, I am inept
To witness it—for it is
>   *Very dark,*
>   *Very dark!*
Since no light is shed…

>   My weary spirit
>   Descends into the
>   Depths of despair.
>   Oh, my hollow heart is
>   Inept to bear love—
>   *How distressing!*

Hitherto, I was gentle,
          Loving,
                  And full of life
But now—now my heart is scorched
From the march of abhorrence, and
While my spirit burns as it flows
Through dark pools of fiery eyes,
My tabescent flesh reveals frail
Brittle bones!
      O' Death, come—
           Take me!

PART II

As the Sun Retires

Diverge!

Her sweet passion,
My violent lust—
Never shall the twain meet
unless…
At the still of the night,
On dark, uninhabited streets.

big beautiful breasts—

Love has no hold
On my dark soul.
    Thirst!
She smiles my way.
She must love me!
    Hunger!
I want her desperately!
I envision my hands
    Tight

Around her waist
FLESH: Yellow haze,
    Creamy White,
       Ginger Brown,
And as black as night!
So soft—So smooth.
I
hunger
  for
    more—
      much more!

Naive lover! Foolish fool!
I reach
  For
    Her
Neck!—
  (She screams!)
Snap!
  Crackle!
    Pop!

Her screams stop!
Her love
  dead
    and
      gone!

City Square

Decrepit shadows hover in the moonlit atmosphere.
These ancient zombies escape putrid
Tombs to stalk the City Square.
Strangers never embrace one another or seem to care
About those whose eye sockets
Possess black festering sores.
Cheeks are ghostly-white and sunken
Like broken eggshells.
Tabescent flesh dangles from marrow-less, brittle bones.
Like slippery saliva, tongues-of-maggots spill
From the wet wombs we politely call mouths. Lone
Beings sing solemn songs among themselves;
Songs of spiritual death and despair with lyrics like:

> I's goin' f-i-i-i-i-ne mah way back ho-o-ome,
> 'Cuz I kin feel it 'n mah bo-o-ones.
> > I won't pick no cot'on, o' tote no ha-a-ayyy,
> > 'Cuz mah ship's done dock't at da ba-a-ayyy.
> I's goin' f-i-i-i-ne mah way back ho-o-ome;
> 'Cuz I kin feel it 'n mah bo-o-ones.

Harmonious hymns are chanted by grim, isolated beings.
They utter words in a call-and-response fashion:

> I's goin' f-i-i-i-ne mah way back ho-o-ome;
> 'Cuz I kin feel it 'n mah bo-o-ones.
> > Da Lord's goin' lead me all da wa-a-ayyy.
> > When I git's t'eaven I's goin' sta-a-ayyy.
> I's goin' f-i-i-i-ne mah way back ho-o-ome;
> 'Cuz I kin feel it 'n mah bo-o-ones.

Though they sing and clank their chained feet,
Along the roadside they quietly creep.
But, once their sightless eyes view fields of wheat,
Like herds of cattle, some scamper while others leap.
To gather wooden baskets, steel hoes, and scythes.
Kneeling women collect and separate
Sugarcane stalks on their thighs.

On the other side of the street, men
And women admire the huts
They made out of straw, sticks and
Mud; then gaze at naked girls
Performing ancestral dances under the
Glittering stars in the sky. Yet,
They don't see apparitions across the
Street—they don't see their future.

Crocodile Tears

During the day,
A black caiman
Basks with mouth agape.
But at night, at night, it hunts.

While gliding quietly through
The cool Columbian waters,
Only my transparent eyes, snout and
Scaled tail are exposed to the weary eyes
Of my prey. By moving my tail quickly,
Back and forth, I propel myself faster
Through the dark, unforgiving waters to
Sneak up on a bird. Suddenly,
I lunge for this bird! But the sweet taste
Of purple feathers escape my gripping jaws
Unharmed. Hunger drives me wild! So, I
Search for another victim, again. The hunt
Is on! Fortunately, drops of rainfall
Clutter her keen, perceptive view.
My scales blend nicely with the surface

Of the rippling waters, and, oh, I will have my
Dinner tonight! I patiently stalk, oh,
Such a beautifully round doe! She looks
So tender and full. Ah, yes! Yes, by all means,
Drink at the edge of this waterhole, my darling! Ah, yes!
She doesn't even notice me! Arrhhh! Come to
Me, my tasty morsel! (Aaahhh!) There's no need
To struggle! Uhhh! You are defenseless! My sharp,
Elongated fangs will tear into your flesh! You
Cannot str-struggle out of this black ca-caiman's powerful
Jaws and webbed-toe grasp! (Aaahhh!) Your screams of
Agony are useless! They won't change my mind!
Crunch!—Ahhhh! The taste of blood which
Oozes from your veins—Oooohhh!—is so divine!
(Awwwh!) I told you to stop screaming!
I will beg you no longer—*snap*!

The broken neck of the doe hangs loosely between the
Powerful jaws of the hungry black
Caiman, who is fortuitous—
For not only did it capture and ravish
A doe, but it won a prize
As well. The doe's warm, round
Paunch carried a fawn inside.
But, in its frenzy, what could it smell? What could it see?
Nothing! It could only taste and swallow whole it's sweet
Victory…without shedding any crocodile tears.

Cascading Light

Cascading light from fire-lit skies
Casts shadows, which stalk rye
Fields and prairies, over old farm
Houses, lampposts, and old red barns,
Through the woods and streams
Into one's scintillating dreams.

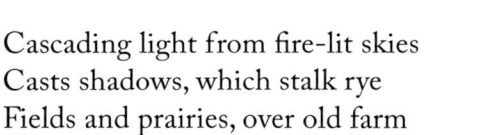

Cascading red light begins to dim,
Thus, the stalking shadows begin to grin!
Their seething souls await dull
Stars to plunder centuries-old souls
Buried in dark infested graves within
Forests, so bodiless spirits can awaken!

Fragments of light from a luminous white moon
Reveal ageless spirits, whose foul fumes loom
Over forlorn wooden caskets. Trees sway low
To avoid sharp scythes swung by wicked shadows.
Rabbits, yearlings, and bear cubs cry tears of horror,
As death kisses the dark lips of their mothers!

Upon the sun's radiant return, where
Once flourishing forests are now bare,
Shadows quickly vanquish into thin air. Many
Green shrubs have been tossed or blown away!
Redwoods have been chopped down to a stump!
Trees stripped of crimson-yellow leaves are dumped

Near Pine trees, black from soot,
Which were burned by liquid flames.
Red and snowy owls' habitats
(Destroyed by chainsaws and blades!)
Are no longer for nature's keeps!
Now weeping willows really weep!

Whispers of the Wild

While walking through the woods,
Beneath my feet I hear the crackling
Of dead leaves and dry sprigs. Thousands
Of insects flee from my enormous being.

No other noises do I hear—
But the dull hooves of gentle reindeer,
The huge brown grizzly paws raking bark off trees,
And the hum of a hive of bees.

And the whispers—whispers of the wild.

As I continue to walk along,
I feel the bite of a bitter wind
That scurries through the forest,
Like a pack of wild, hungry wolves.

The wandering wind forces the limbs of trees
To scrape the solid cold ground.
I hasten my pace for fear of losing my face
And bruising my beautiful crown.

There again are the whispers—whispers of the wild.

Behind me I hear a crackling!
I turn my head and there I see
A blur of something gray falling—
Wham! It hit the cold, solid ground before me.

A precious little baby bird struggles alone;
No mother bird to retrieve it, no guardian to take it home.
Dare I resume my speedy steps, or shall I embrace this pet
And return this poor bird back to its nest?

Would nature truly be as caring as I?
Would it forsake this timid creature, to do or die?
Perhaps! Perhaps not! So, I reach out my large mittens
To shield this soft, downy bird, like its former shell.

Oh, gracious, gracious me!
From which tree did fall thee?
Must I scale each tree and risk a fall,
For the whispers of the wild do howl!

I turn my head to see.
I strain my ears to hear
The sounds that seem so near,
But the whispers of the wild are far away.

Before the sun retires and the moon resumes its post,
The whispers of the night beckon me. I, with my
Little, cuddly, downy friend, hasten my step most
Expediently! Although the moon can illuminate the sky,

The whispers of the wild can darken the forest
And cause strangers in this wooded area to cry,
Like all those before who have wept.
All I wish is for my new friend and I not to die!

As the Sun Retires

As the sun retires and the moon resumes its post,
Four-legged devils stir at night.
They move swiftly like packs of hungry ghosts,
At a constant pace and flight.
These raving mad predators search for a host
For their party. Suddenly, a host is in sight!
A pregnant brown doe is tired and lost.
She is paralyzed with intense fright
Once she sees their menacing grins
And their snarling yellow teeth.
The ghostly pack surround her, then move in for the kill.
The terrified doe, with one last breath,
Bellows in the woods to no avail.
Daggers for claws and needles for teeth
Rip the deer's skeleton from its corporeal
Self, like a knife from its sheath!
Within its former mother's womb, a fawn struggles.

Aware of this, one of the viscous white wolves
Rakes its fangs across the brown fawns neck, until
It no longer wiggles with life. The wolves' foul breaths
Hover in the air tonight, like the scent of death.

PART III

Many Moons Ago

Wars

For centuries, nations of men—
Whether tribal or communal—
Have forsaken the Holy Spirit to
Listen to malign, diabolical
Voices of their egos, and, thus, pursue
Territorial conquests…
                Instead of peace!

Caesar's perilous lot has captured our beloved King!
War has thus begun! Perhaps I
Should learn Roman things,
Like how to fluently speak their native tongue?—
                Et tu, Brute!

Unconsciously, wavering pictures of
Death—red, white, and blue
Fragmented skeletons poorly clothed
In strips of dripping dark-hue
Skin—are envisioned. I awake in the midst of
                a civil war!

A Marine and Nazi soldier waltz hand-in-hand
Under the moonlight, until death takes its silent turn and
One is left nervously grinning and gravely
                standing alone.

Hoards of camouflaged gear and black
Boots walk across miles of hot jungle,
Surrounded by explosives and the
Vietcong, who fight for control
Of their land, (which was ours to claim);
But we return home shunned and
                empty-handed.

Bosnian soldiers tirelessly battle
Serbian forces for territory
They choose not to share; but instead
Force citizens to innocently
Drink from the well of anger, dismay, poverty,
                and despair!

Rwandan Hutus rebel against their own kind.
And Tutsi's (the sightless) really lead the blind!
Instead, they should build a nation of strong
                Africans!

Death seeps into festering wounds to imbibe the red
Hue which flows through vascular
Tubes. Translucent blood
Appears as liquid crystals on tan, swarthy, pale, and
                Dust-stained cheeks.

Number A2234

While we storm through Auschwitz,
We are intrigued by the
Mysterious snow that falls from clear
Skies; and once we reach
The Polish ghettos, we infiltrate the halls of many
Slum-lord apartments. A truly horrible acrid stench
Sickens me, as we tread lightly in boots up dire stairs
Polluted with the remains of an old man's body.
Tattered clothes poorly and grossly conceal obscure
Bruises, scars, and markings on ghostly skin. Dark red dye
Stains his mouth, neck, and short
Brown hair. As I examine
His tabescent flesh, cracked ribs suddenly stretch forth!
Rotten, yellow teeth are overdue for a good scrubbing.
By the firm nylon bristles of Dupont's toothbrush.
Cold frightened and frozen eyes, as white as the sky,
Are sunken deep into hollow shell-
Like sockets. Stamped only

On his chest is serial number A2234. *Oh, my!*
Atrocities of war and genocide can never be
Erased! Oh, if only he had been on *Schindler's List*,
Perhaps parched lips would not have
Tasted death's bitter kiss.

Wa-Tu Wa-Le Wa-Mefika

A brown baby suckles the nurturing juices
From the drooping tit of her mother
A thirsty warrior yearns the soft cool water
Cradled in his dusty hands; however, he uses
His patriarchal hands to feed
The water to the craving parched lips of a child

    "Wa-tu wa-le wa-mefika!"
"Those people have arrived!" screams the village idiot.
    "Wa-tu wa-le wa-mefika!"
Eyes, white with fright, express immense danger.

Everyone ignores him and continues
To perform their dance of life.

    "Wa-tu wa-le wa-mefika!"
"Those people have arrived!" The
Village idiot screams again.
    "Wa-tu wa-le wa-mefika!"
Eyes exploding with intense white fright!

In the distance, the clinking and
Clanking of metal armor can
Be heard among the explosive sounds
Of huge black cannons.
The chief begins to stir from his straw lair. his harem
Stands behind his broad bronze shoulders. Yet, his brawn
And bravery will be outmatched by
Huge European armies—
The Dutch, English, French, Spanish, and Portuguese.

    "Wa-tu wa-le wa-mefika!"
A conquistador aims a dusty musket
At the village idiot and fires.
    "Wa-tu wa-le wa-mefika!"
A pellet lodges in the back of the village
Idiot's head, and he falls dead.

My people fling their naked spears
Toward the heads of white demons.
If only Gueno, the African god with
All His wrath, could descend at dusk
To defeat the imperial skulls-of-death,
White like elephant tusks.

Teary black and brown eyes sparkle like wet sand, whilst
Green and blue eyes reflect sunrays like tinted skyscrapers.
Swarthy hands are clasped together in the form of ancient

Egyptian pyramids. like baobab tree branches, bony fingers
Reach toward heaven's midday stars
To summon ancient spirits.

    "Wa-tu wa-le wa-mefika!"
Everyone now screams in frantic unison!
    "Wa-tu wa-le wa-mefika!"
Anarchy climbs their spineless backs of fear!

(Aldo do Espinto Santo cries as he sings with fervor:
"And the blood of lives fallen/ in the forest of death/
innocent blood/ drenching the earth/ in a silence of terrors/
shall make the earth fruitful/ crying for justice")

A hot breeze slowly collects clusters
Of dust, which hover around
The shuffling heels of many African kings and queens,
Like pesky gnats swarming around the
Tail of a nervous gazelle. Herds
Of human cattle stalk the arid grasslands under the arches
Of muskets into floating wooden dungeons,
Headed for the new world.

Still, high above the majestic purple escarpment of the
Ahaggar and snowcapped Kilimanjaro mountains;
Way beyond acres of glebes, full of wheat and maize;
Clear across the dry Muhabi, Sahara, and Kalahari deserts,
And millenniums before this time.

A tapestry of African ancestry, with the soles of their feet
Woven into the sun-baked earth,
Dance to the rhythm of life:
My people shake, stamp, jerk, and step to the beat of life.
Thus, the efficacy of a rain dance—they sprinkle water on
The ground and, with happy hands, raise
Their gourd bowls to the sun.
Then soft pattering feet swiftly erupt
Into a thunderous fury—

    Dance, jungle lords—
        Dance! Dance!
Dance your mimetic and esoteric dances.

My people sing with tongues rich
In dialect and language.
    Sing, jungle lords—
        Sing! Sing!
My people, sing out! like the endangered bald eagle;
Shout loud, so that your voices will
Be heard in the passing wind,
So that other nations will one day say
Of us: "Wa-tu wa-le wa-mefika!"

Weeping Willow

On an unusually hot summer morn',
Half-naked I hang from an old brown
Wooden beam in an old Confederate barn.
My ebony bare back, so muscular and brawn,

Awaits the agonizing pain
That I must endure once again
My Massah swings his cracklin'
Whip to land upon jet-black skin.

The air, the slithery black whip does forsake,
Lands with the stinging bite of a rattlesnake!
The two-tongued whip rips off my African flesh,
Like dead bark yanked off a sacred oak tree.

From the shock of the leather sword,
Red reams of blood squirt forward,
Trickling down my blistering back

(As Langston's, "dusky rivers, like
The Euphrates and Nile") straight into a huge
Red sea upon my blood-stained pants to converge.
Ohhh this! My cruel punishment! For catching the
Cool taste of shade beneath a weeping willow tree.

Many Moons Ago

Here upon Mother Earth's lap I sit,
With my auburn legs crossed like that of a
Hopi Chief, who summons ancient spirits
To protect his humble pueblos each day
From wars waged by the Navajo and Apache—
(Whom he wishes to love instead of hate)
Like a Squaw, I await warm energy
From the golden sphere's rays; I await
The morning tears of heaven's angels
That will rapidly fall and quickly burst
Into thousands of tiny, wet crystals;
And graciously nourish Mother Earth's crust.
I, a warrior, wait for the silver moon
To illuminate winter white shadows
Who slowly stalk our native land too soon!
Without regards to the hawk and sparrow's
Cries, they cast many moons into the teeth
Of a bitter wind! Now the wind and rain

And sun and moon have convinced Mother Earth
To forsake us! *The past we can't regain!*
> The shrills of the fretful hawk and sparrow
> Echo faintly in the valley below.

January 8, 1994

PART IV

A Candle Lit Above the Trees

The Sun Sets on Many Hearts

If you must leave,
Then leave me!—
>   But do not take the rising sun;

Do not take the warm, subtle, tickling
Yellow feathers of the golden bird.
If you must leave, then please hush—
>   Leave without a single word.

If you must go,
Then go with the warm southern wind,
As do birds once Jack Frost sings.
Leave behind the harsh Arctic winds—
>   But do not return in spring!

If you must leave,
Then leave me alone as if the setting sun, yet
To drape red tears over western hills, like many
Men before me who have wept!
Leave me if you must, lady—
>   But long before the scintillant sun sets.

Shattered Heart

Blood ceaselessly leaks from her heart until
Its cavities are emptied and dried. Afterward, pieces
Of her fragmented heart crumble and fall into a pile
Of rubbish. A gentle breeze sweeps the abandoned pile
Into a corner for safekeeping, but it's too late, she is
Heartless and cold! Beseeched by darkness!
Some of her humanly senses have either
Altered or perished. She feels not with her
Heart but with her timid mind. To her, the air
Is no longer perfumed by laurels and attar;
However, smells like a grave of putrid leaves
Which fall from disgruntled and forsaken trees.
Her lips no longer savor the flavor of fine wines,
However worships the acrid taste of sour grapes.
Before her dull eyes, beauty appears in the image
Of green gargoyles affixed to the sky's obscure collage.
In her world, darkness squeezes light out of
The sky, like water rung from a damp cloth.
That light drips over western hills and is absorbed

By the cold, cold earth—if she could have only bathed
In the dawn's early raining light, maybe she would
Have been able to slowly collect her shattered
Heart off the floor and place it back inside
Her vacant bosom for safekeeping.

Little Bluebird

A little bluebird pecks at my windowpane.

Little bird, sing sweet songs—
Do chirp all morn' long.
>With your soft, ruffled plumage
>And your bright yellow beak—
>You are mild,
>You are mild and meek.

Little bird, sing sweet, strong songs—
Do chirp all morn' long.
>For shallow is the sound of my voice.
>Words which I chatter by choice
>Do not spring forth from my lips
>As lucidly as morning dew

Falls upon the leaves of grass.

Yet, like each blade of grass that inhales human breath,
>I do breathe the earthly mist of nature's open skies;

Yet I do blossom like the glistening flowers

> After April showers, and fall on occasion
> Like the lonely leaves of autumn;

Yet I do feel with my mind as well as with my heart.
> *But why doesn't my voice penetrate the air?*
> *Why do my awful sounds (words from my throat)*
> *Possess nothing but stolidity in flight?*

Yet why do I, without wings, stir passionately upon
> The earth, chirp like a boisterous bird,
> But sound faint in the wind?
> Then fall godforsaken upon solemn shores.

Dear little bluebird,
> Sing soulful, stirring songs!
> Do chirp—*chirp for me*—all night long.

Lieben

I alone on my island,
Sat patiently watching the sands
Of time wash away into the mouth of the sea.
Suddenly, where there is a break between the
Sky and sea, a speck of blue danced
Merrily before my eyes.
While hovering over big greenish-
Blue waters in the cloudy sky,
This dark speck emerged as a bluebird
Which perched itself upon my shoulders, then whispered
Strange words in my ear; words
That I had never heard:
"Lieben," the little bluebird gently said
As a frown of dread crossed my forehead.
"Amor!" it shouted at me.
I shunned it away and turned back to the sea.
"Amore!" it steadily cried.
So I glanced at the petulant bird,
Shrugged my shoulders and sighed.
It peered passionately at me with worried

Eyes. This flustered and brokenhearted creature,
Unfortunately with broken spirit, had to endure
A salty sea that streamed from its sullen eyes.
Suddenly and completely to my surprise,
"L-o-v-e," from its yellow beak it muttered,
As its soft blue wings hysterically fluttered.
Into the horizon it drifted away without loves reprieval,
And into the teeth of a bitter wind.
     Surprisingly, I was dismayed
And perturbed by this bird,
     Because I still did not know
What the bird had wanted.
        "Wait, wait, little bluebird!" I exclaimed.
          "What is l-o-v-e?"

A Candle Lit Above the Trees

As the congregation
Approaches the altar
To witness or feel a spiritual sign,
They are compelled
By their hearts of gold
To reveal their sinful crimes.

As they bend
To their knees for prayer,
To some, something marvelous occurs.
Disciples are now in
Touch with God's lair.
He has quenched their spiritual thirsts.

While a few elite
Rise to their feet,
Others kneel soundlessly still.
They have been summoned
To higher ground.
They are now free from all ills.

For those who
Remain standing on earth will,
Out of pity and awe, fall back to their knees.
Though their hearts and souls do
Suffer, they fail to realize there is still
A candle lit above the trees.

PART V

She Drank from My Cup

She Drank from My Cup

She drank from my cup,
> Like no other before her.
She ate from my hands,
> Like a yearling with delight!

From her cup I drank,
> Because I adored her!
But the drink was poisoned,
> And from her cup I sank.

Above my body she hovered
> With a sharp, curved dagger gleaming in the light!
She sliced and tore open my chest!
> Then stole my heart like a phantom in the night!

A Steady Beat

My heart once beat like a drum,
Full of rhythm—
>A steady beat.
>A steady beat.

But because my poor soul suffered
From a relationship I once was in,
My ideas, thoughts, and feelings
Were unarranged and rhythmless—
Scattered wildly in my brain!
The musical undertones were insane!
Unleashed was a tempestuous storm
That affected my nervous heart.

Now my heart no longer beats like a drum,
Full of rhythm—
>A steady beat.
>A steady beat.

That love I had for her
Was too damn deep!

Valentine's Forgotten Memory

Although many Valentine's Day memories have been
Slowly dissolved within my vast soul long ago,
Still no new flow tides come ashore to ebb away
The horrible images etched in the sands of time
As intrinsically as Albrecht Durer's *Praying Hands*.

No warmth is near to ease the pain
Of yesteryear's bitter winds.
Yet although waves of emotions for her
Stir tempestuously within me,
My eyes remain dry; no rain trickles down my face!
I push back the immense tide of images near the horizon
With assistance from the gods' cosmic forces.

I myself can handle the colossal
Dimensions of my cluttered soul:
Distance—how far can I separate my heart and soul;
Depth—how deep can I bury my darkest secrets and sins;
And time—the dark figure that can never be chained—

Lurks through muddy souls and constantly
Sails through previously chartered waters
To force us to reminisce about
    A Valentine's forgotten memory.

She Is Not My Wife

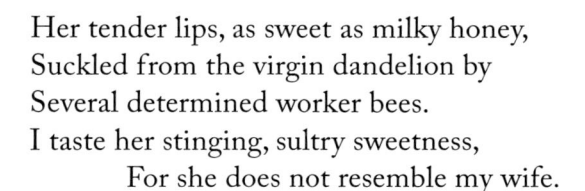

Her tender lips, as sweet as milky honey,
Suckled from the virgin dandelion by
Several determined worker bees.
I taste her stinging, sultry sweetness,
      For she does not resemble my wife.

Hair, short and silky, smells of attar;
Hair, long and flowing like a golden river.
I must lie in this river's bed again,
To release the tension trapped within,
      For she does not resemble my wife.

Skin as soft as rose petals merges with mine!
Adjoined, are we, upon blades of soft, yellow-green
Beneath an apple tree. After I am consumed by
Her sultry womb, she rests while I reach for a juicy
Apple to eat. I eat, sit, and stare at her loveliness;
I smile from ear to ear at her pure, winsome nakedness!
      For she does not resemble my wife.

The sun is not as hot as she, nor the
Heavy breeze scented with natural musk;
And if this breeze is really lust that I breathe,
Then I'll even inhale its torrid air at dusk!
     For she does not resemble my wife.

Remnants of Sex

Streaky red lines are etched on a face that's
Covered with splashes of pain.
Reflecting misery like a spectrum reflects the color blue.

Dark circles have beseeched sleepy brown eyes;
Big puffy eyes refuse to open wide.
An uneasy smile fails to light up an already dim face.

Soft, silky skin is bruised beyond repair.
Plum-sweet lips are now cracked and bitter-dry.
She reeks of an alcohol-like perfume; she smells as though
She has bathed all night long in a large pool of Colt 45.

The remnants of sex, violent sex, stifle the summer breeze.
Although she shutters with fright, I hope she put up a good fight.

June 27, 1995

She Sits Quiet and Still

She sits quiet and almost still
In a corner of His lustrous room,
Curled up like a blue ball
And inflated with dark gloom.
Eyes as puffy as a blowfish
And as red as the setting sun,
Gaze deeply into the eyes
      Of His only begotten Son.

Knees locked tighter than a vice grip,
Because her body aches of forced love
      From the shadow of the cloth.

The sinister shadow puts
On his cloak and white collar.
Then floats over from the pulpit
And places his hand upon her
Shoulder. He hands her rosemary
Beads, then utters a chaplain's
Prayer to cleanse his soul and says,
      "The Lord forgives all earthly sins."

Pale cheeks are drained
Of life,
And full of despair.
Anguish is etched in her brow
From the pain of incisors and molars
Which ripped out her hair.
Her strife
Is never claimed.

Blue eyes, distant as the
Horizon—
But not as beautiful.

June 29, 1996

To Mock the Raven

Dark ebony eyes turn white with terror.
Panicked lungs breathe heavier
And faster, at times, gasping for air.
While wild legs fling forever—
But move no more than an inch—silent
Screams of terror are like trees that
Fall in a forest, and if not seen,
Then are never heard. At sixteen
She was still precious, merely a virgin.
But to mock Poe's, *The Raven*,
The rapist declares, "Nevermore, nevermore…"
(Words that her subconscious will often recur).

June 27, 1996

Shimmering Blue Eyes

Darkness encircles her swollen eyes.
Shimmering water-blue eyes
The shade of teary-eyed skies,
A casual color as cool
As a dip in a backyard pool.
One would definitely find
Peace in lovely languid liquid
Eyes of baby blue.

Clear skin once as smooth as velvet
Is now covered with jagged cuts.
Beautifully polished fingernails
Colored with rainbow designs reveal
Torn skin underneath. Blue bruises
Creep up inner thighs toward a dark fortress—
That damn delicate lock has been
Hideously broken…

I wish again to kiss those soft
Red lips, which once oozed with
Strawberry-sweet juices. Although
Mesmerized by two drops of crystal-
Blue water, my muscles ache
From hands cuffed behind my back;
Still, I kneel down to steal a kiss
From cold, bloodstained lips.

June 5, 1997

PART VI

Purple Prisms of Pain

Possession

A glass-pipe dream
Cooks before me,
The effervescence of death stirs
Within my veins.
My illusory world rises
Swiftly, and with similar speed,
Comes crashing
Down upon my troubled
Soul and constricts
The flow of red waters
Through coarse channels.
For years my prickly nerves
Have been sheared by
Paranoia while balancing
Themselves on a thin wire.

I can hear the cries
Echoing…echoing…
"Daddy, please don't go!
Please stay home with me!"

But who has time to
Listen to voices with
No faces. No mirror
Can reflect wet crystals
Twinkling in the
Eyes of the innocent.
Yet voices
Ricochet off every
Corner of my house
And carry with it the
Forlorn cries of society.
A glass-pipe dream
Beckons me to fulfill it.
Swarthy skin yearns for
A drop of calomine or aloe vera,
But instead welcomes cold metal
As it pierces the inner walls
Of my godforsaken temple,
And flushes poison
Throughout my entire being.

June 5, 1997

Please Don't Go!

"Billy, Billy!" they called to me.
But I simply could not respond.
I watched their frantic eyes
And knew they'd do me no harm.

I tried to utter a word or two
But my voice was surely faint.
My throat felt dry, my tongue numb,
And my heart beat like a slow drum.

My loving mother grabbed her face
To hide her silent tears as
Dad pressed upon my chest
To force me to inhale the stale air.

Slowly my vision began to fade.
But, I could faintly hear my
Sister pleading with me—
"Billy, don't give up! Please, don't go!"

Yet I could not grant her that wish.
Although I could taste the stale air on my tongue,
It was extremely hard to breathe with
A four-inch switchblade puncturing my lungs.

As I closed my eyes, all I could see
Was a white cloud hovering above me.
I reached for that cloud and never looked back
At the life that I lead, before I was attacked.

Distant Sounds of Drunken Laughter

Distant sounds of drunken laughter
Reverberate along the halls of my mind.
It grows in volume—it grows higher
And higher into a loud, screaming, blind
Pitch! Nooo!

My eyes burn like red-hot pokers! I rub
My eyes, but the burning continues! My hands
Are wet and red…red and wet…and red
My clothes smell of nervous sweat and
Perfume—sweet, subtle perfume—
I stumble to the floor from
The weight of my burden.

The red blaze leaps off crackling logs as shimmering
Shadows creep along the walls and ceiling.
I can see my hands trembling in the burning light
The burning flame flickers like a fading candlelight.
As I kneel over my sweet fallen angel.

Future Becomes Present Becomes Past

      In time, future becomes present becomes past…
A turbulent tide rolls
Forward as its undercurrent
Rolls backward.
      The cycle never breaks, never tires

      The future echoes the present echoes the past…
Putrid, pulpy mass
Rotted by maggots that
Infested its core relinquishes
      Its journeyman spirit,

While

      Spiritless scavengers roam earth

In search of elixirs and natural
Herbal tranquilizers.
Death stalks the surging ship
    Of spirits that struggle

Against turbulent tides

June 24, 1998

Eyes Closed to the Light

Ears closed to the light
Stroke of violin strings
That
Echo the solemn tears of angels.

Eyes deaf to the gentle
Caress of harp strings
That
Echo the voice of serenity.

Smiling lips hum the
Sweet sounds of soprano saxophones
That
Echo the cool notes of jazz.

Hearts beat with the rhythm
Of opening
And closing
Heaven's gates.

Music is the only escape
From the torrid reality of death.

July 26, 1998

Reflection

As he peers into the shiny silver mirror
He is only a shadow of his former self,
A worm trapped in a dark shell—
As forgotten as the "Invisible Man;"
Even more so since his own kind fails
To recognize his sorrow…his hurt…his pain.
To them he is still the same joker
Who can create funny anecdotes at whim;
But these jokes are the sergeant-at-arms
That protect his hidden tears, preventing
Them from falling like the Berlin Wall.
For a moment, in his trembling hands could
One see the reflected image of a frightened
Child emerge from a tired old man's sad face.
Yet as he slides the sharp serrated mirror
Back and forth, a cold red river spreads over his image
And hides the lonely child within forevermore.

July 25, 1995

I Was Born Not Out of Love

I was born not out of love
        but of…
Purple pain and pure pleasure
Tossed into an obscure
Pot of hot Cajun despair.
Lonely nights hunger
Company of any kind.
Meek eyes are destined
To stare into bloodstained eyes
And intermingle for
One night, for one kiss of bliss,
Beneath the naked stars.

I was born not out of love
        but of…
Shameful submission to "Dr. Feelgood"
On a hot, sticky night, reeking
Of nervous alcoholic fervor. "Dr. Feelgood"
Uses its nonsterile syringe
To penetrate subcutaneous

Tissues and inject fluids of miraculous
Energy into an unyielding cavity,
During the dark hue of night.
Just before it withdraws bloody
Love, whimpering sounds take flight.

I was born not out of love
       but of…
Screams of unforsaken terror
Scratch lead-painted walls
And leap through windowpanes for
Fear of mistakes so small,
Like cracked lips speaking out.
Choked and muffled words shout
Through angry hands, as sore eyes moan
And swell from less anguish
Than bitterly broken bones.

If I was not born out of love,
       then why was I born?

July 12, 1998

Purple Prisms of Pain

A well of sorrow swells up in her bosom
Before overflowing.
Tender strands of sorrow leave tiny streaks upon
A weary face,

> Thus revealing
> > Contours of misery,
>
> And reflecting
> > Purple prisms of pain…

Her moaning startles a sparrow clinging
To a branch in a nearby tree; and
Causes the sparrow's frozen wings
To shatter into tiny pieces of glass.

> Thus revealing
> > Contours of misery,
>
> And reflecting
> > Purple prisms of pain…

She kneels down to the cold earth
        And carefully picks up the
Broken wings of the bird.
She gently wipes cold white dust from its feathers
        And steadily tends to the
Sparrow, unaware that it is dead.

        Thus revealing
                Contours of misery,
      And reflecting
                Purple prisms of pain…

She raises her trembling arms, as long
As grapevines, toward heaven,
And in return, angelic hands touch
The aching heart of a mother.
How she longs to say "good-bye" once again
Since she often forgot to say "hello" to her
Only begotten son.

January 13, 1997

PART VII

Beyond the Blue Moon

Crescendo

The trumpet's tantalizing tunes reverberate
Like the lusty call of a sparrow's mate.
The soft yet crisp sounds of the flute
Whistle like a cool coastal wind's toot—
      Swooping up, swooping down,
      Speeding up, slowing down;
And lingers at the earliest of dawn,
Like the scent of freshly-cut orchids.
As if roses, submersed in liquid oxygen, they do
Drink the sun's warm rays. Men and women too
Absorb florescent red rays while engrossed by the sweet,
Sultry sounds of the tenor saxophone. In concert,
Mesmerized heads move to the rhythm and beat
Of fluid notes—
      Swooping up, swooping down
      Speeding up, slowing down;
That linger in the midnight air.

Sand and Pebble

Rolling waves of green wash ashore my dreams
Of yesteryear's, it seems, old fading dreams.
I scoop up a handful of sand and pour
It into my left hand. A pool of sand—a mere
Ocean of vast land on which I travel,
On which I stand with dreams to unravel.
I reach for a pebble near my right foot
Like a polished basketball star, I shoot
The blue quartz into the immense
Rolling blue-green waters.
It skips once across the surface and quickly disappears.
Like that pebble, I too am blue and have gaily skipped
Across tough waters once or twice but always drowned.
And like the sand I toss into a gusting breeze, indeed,
One day as dust, I too will scatter briskly in the breeze.

Silver Shadows

Childish eyes innocently descry
Angels among the swarming clouds,
While trees struggle with the bitter breeze by,
Pressing their limbs against the cold ground.
As a bluish-silver streak flashes in the sky
With an electrifying and thunderous
Force, rainbow tears drip from the swollen eyes
Of somber white clouds like falling prisms.
Obscure shadows of the day drift by like the wind.
By dusk, mysterious silver shadows and soon
Silhouettes creep and crawl over the earth, even
Underneath the watchful eyes of the luminous moon.
Like dazzling diamonds or white gold's glare,
Silver souls sparkle in the swirling midnight air.

January 8, 1994

Verlanda—You Were Taken Much Too Soon

You rest so peacefully on white satin cushions, in
Your ebony casket. You appear as if Michelangelo
Himself molded you from brown clay and pinned
Your little golden wings to your sides…
>You were taken away
>From us too soon,
>>Much too soon!

When I think of how the sun would gaily
Dance in the air like fluttering
Black butterflies that would quickly
Reveal the golden-yellow undersides of their wings…
>You were taken away
>From us too soon,
>>Much too soon!

Now, yellow tears drip from the eyes of the sun upon
Your grave, watering the lilies and white roses
That we planted and laid near your tombstone
Long ago. Take these gifts to God, my young goddess…
    You were taken away
    From us too soon,
        Much too soon!
            My darling angel.

January 8, 1994

Verlanda 2—If You'd Known Her

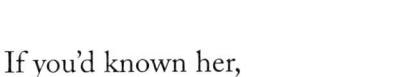

If you'd known her,
You would know love.
You can't picture
How much I miss her so.

Rain falls from skies
Easier than
Water rung from a cloth,
But not as rapidly
As tears well up in my eyes.

I miss her when
The wind swings on
Old tree limbs in
The country, or even

When the wind plays
kick the can down
A quiet surburban
Street or sings beautiful
Nursery rhymes with nightingales.

The rain consoles
Me when its paws
Pounce upon my old rooftop.
Its purr drowns out my

Silent screams,
Cool autumn air
Embraces my lonely
Horrid thoughts, and moisture
Hides my waterlogged dreams.

I love her so.
Yet only God
Knows my Verlanda and
How much I miss her so.

January 13, 1997

River of Light

    At first,
All it seems to do
Is creep through
My windowpane.
    But soon,
Its wondrously scintillant
Rays of hope dissolve remnants
Of piercing purple pain
As surreal nightmares
Fade like centuries
Into the coolness of autumn.

        Rustling tangerine
    And crimson
    Leaves glisten beneath the
    Bright orb and scamper from the wind.

    Pastel
Colors drip across
Monet's "Lillies
in the Pond."

        but soon,
As if a lone male lion
With a sweeping yellow mane,
It flees from my bedroom.
Tall thickets hide its glow,
Leaving no more naked shadows
To dance upon the leaves of grass.

              By dusk, the shaded
        Glow of
        Candlelight soon fades
        Into its darkest hour,

And abandons me.

        Dear blue moon,
Please emerge from your eerie tomb
And cast your dim light of gloom
Upon a pained heart.
        Please, fair moon,
 Shine your luminous river
Of light on a sullen creature
Who yearns the warmth of June
But will surely settle
For the moderately cool,
Soothing touch of a companion.

January 10, 1997

Beyond the Blue Moon

As the sun retires, a somber and austere
Sphere glows in the distance, smeared
Against a dark-gray background,
    Like a lonely teardrop stain on a love letter.

    Luminescent craters for eyes cast blue shadows
    Along the edge of dense forests and
        At the mouths of blue lakes,

And the blue moon's light

    Brilliantly beams from its celestial being,
    Pulling high and low tides toward sanguine shores
        Of quiet beach fronts.

Perhaps a utopian milieu really exists on the moon
Or in the metaphysical—a place free of crime, pollution,
Nuclear waste, deadly diseases, death, and
Overpopulation—
    A place beyond the blue moon…

Where rainbows sparkle in the winter skies;
Where grass never bleeds yellow thirst and
   Grows tall in spring like green glass towers;

Beyond the blue moon…

   Where butterflies blossom like begonias and dandelions.
   Where june bugs resemble neon signs outside nightclubs and
   Billiards that often brighten the night sky.

A place millenniums and galaxies away from
The everyday struggles of teenaged welfare moms
And deadbeat dads, who try to forget
Their starving children.
     A place beyond the blue moon.